FINDING
WORK–LIFE
BALANCE

FINDING
WORK–LIFE
BALANCE

Achieving Fulfilment at
Every Stage of Life

JOS VAN DER BRUG

Floris Books

Translated by Eduard van der Maas

First published in Dutch by Christofoor Publishers
under the title *Levenfasen en werk: Coachen, leidinggeven, teamwork*

First published in English in 2015 by Floris Books

MIX
Paper from
responsible sources
FSC® C117931

 This book is also available as an eBook

British Library CIP Data available
ISBN 978-178250-166-4

Printed & Bound by MBM Print SCS Ltd, Glasgow

Contents

The Social Stage

The Different Stages
of Life and Work

> In a lifetime we get one period to learn, one to struggle,
> and one to become wise. What comes thereafter is a gift
> from the gods: *then* we may enjoy life.
>   – Ancient Chinese proverb

This rough division of life into four stages contains a lot of truth, but it misses a crucial detail. While work may feel at times like a burden, we should be able to find enjoyment *throughout* our lives – not just when we retire! This book is about helping us find the balance in our working and private lives as they change throughout the years.

The proverb can however be extremely useful in understanding how we can achieve that balance as we learn, struggle and become wise. This is an underlying sequence we all tend to follow, no matter how diverse our lives may seem.

Youth is undoubtedly marked by learning. Not just learning in school, but also learning to relate to people and to the world around us. Young minds soak up influence from everyone they associate with – parents, teachers and many others.

Then, in the first stage of adulthood, people scramble to find their place in the world. A job, a family, a circle of friends, an income, a position – these don't come automatically. Whether we like it or not, we must struggle to overcome every kind of obstacle that lies between where we are and where we want to be.

Sooner than we think, we will eventually feel that we have accomplished (at least outwardly) all we can achieve. Perhaps we had wanted more; perhaps we are satisfied. But in this period many people will question what meaning they will give to the later part of their life. Dealing with this question can indeed bring wisdom.

So, where does enjoyment come into the equation? In our ageing population, retirement is being pushed further and further back, so we need to bring life and work into balance along the way to reach that goal. Our inner attitude is vital in this – we can accumulate joy, peace and wisdom on our journey, or we can gather up regret, guilt and resentment.

Just as important is the way we relate to others and work in teams. It goes without saying that when we collaborate we must consider each individual's various qualities and talents. But too few of us also consider where each person is on their life's journey. The 40-year-old accountant in the next office was once a child of 5 and will become an elderly person of 80. She remains the same person, but changes drastically in the course of her life, both inwardly and outwardly. Being aware of our colleagues' work-life stages can enhance their lives as much as our own.

As many traditions have done before, the anthroposophical view following Rudolf Steiner divides life into cycles of seven years. This is based on observations that each period of seven years has unique, distinct elements that characterise that part of our journey. The first of these is the seven years prior to losing our milk-teeth, where physical growth abounds, followed by another seven year burst in cognitive, analytical growth.

This small book describes each stage of working life and outlines the capacities and potential pitfalls we are likely to experience in each one, especially as regards our relationship to work. By understanding these stages, we can better achieve balance between our work and our private lives. This method builds on the work of Bernard Lievegoed, who inspired a generation of professionals in the sixties.

Each chapter includes a case study to illustrate and explore real-life problems and possibilities, and frequent tips will help both employees and employers find practical ways to understand and address the role of age within their organisation. What does each stage of life offer in the composition of a team? What must managers pay attention to in their coaching? How can we best approach someone who isn't coping at work? And how might our life stage be affecting the different challenges we face?

A word of warning

The Chinese expression which introduces this book, as well as its further divisions into seven-year stages, indicate that the various periods in our lives each have a predictable colour and quality. However, all kinds of circumstances affect the development of our lives – what some people gain in their twenties, others do not acquire until they are in their forties, and vice versa. This doesn't mean that there is anything wrong with people who don't fit the mould – it is in deviations from the pattern that we see the uniqueness of every life.

Characterising the various stages of life therefore brings with it the danger of labelling. This happens when, on the basis of a few casual observations, people are quickly slotted into a life stage and the characteristics that belong to that stage are attributed to them.

The model presented here is not intended to classify or categorise in that way – we are all unique. But our understanding can be sharpened when we look with care through the lenses of these life stages. Doing so can help us find the appropriate balance in our own working lives, which will in turn enrich and deepen our understanding and compassion towards others in the workplace and at home.

The Receptive Stage

1. Childhood and Adolescence: 0–21

The rapidly forming character

This chapter is a little less detailed than the rest, as the main focus of this book is on working life. It would be unwise, however, to neglect this vitally important stage as we all carry elements of our childhood development throughout life.

What makes this stage unique?

Lievegoed calls this learning period the 'receptive' stage, and with good reason. Young people don't just grow physically: during these three seven-year cycles, incredible psychological and spiritual development also takes place. Children are open to the influence of their environment, parents and educators, and will use every experience to equip themselves for adulthood and independence. Of course, some of their thinking and behavioural habits will be replaced, modified or discarded later in life, but by age 21, individuals are essentially set up for life.

Some lessons that will be taken into later life are:

▶ **The rulebook:** Children tend to unconsciously adopt customs, rules and rituals laid out in the household, in school, in their hobbies, etc. In adulthood, notions about what can and cannot be done at work are often grounded in foundations that were laid in childhood. For example, the rule 'first finish your homework, then you can play' can become a useful work-life habit.

▶ **Creative scope:** The degree to which children learn to use their imagination has a huge impact on their later creativity and point of view. As children, our own expressive and metaphorical capacities are activated during play – a tree trunk can become a castle, the rug can become a deep lake, and we are the clever mouse who always outwits the cat!

▶ **Rebellion:** The balance we find between obedience and wilfulness as children often foreshadows our adult attitude towards authority and our relationships with others. With this 'working balance' set in place, we step into life inclined either to acquiesce or to protest. Some of us may never find this balance, and will find fault with both too little and too much direction at work.

▶ **Dealing with conflict:** The manner in which our parents resolve quarrels often serves as example for how we will later resolve conflicts at work as well as in our homes.

▶ **Convictions and beliefs:** Our overarching view of the world – acquired in childhood – will resonate at work and at home: beliefs may become intensified, or we may react against them in later years. Whether our parents and educators addressed these ideals dogmatically or open-mindedly will also determine how we will later impress our views upon others.

Despite these examples, the receptive stage does not *have* to determine the rest of an individual's life. A view of ourselves as victims, blaming early years for all kinds of current problems, is understandable but unhelpful in the long run.

As adults, it is useful to unpack the 'suitcase' of our childhood, to form our own judgment about what is inside, and to find a healthy way to relate to it. It might even be possible for some of us to re-pack the suitcase having discarded certain items, and to move on with lighter baggage! Because our childhood and teenage years have such influence, it can sometimes be profitable for the development of a team if the members feel comfortable enough to share stories about their youth.

The Expansive Stage

2. Our Twenties: 21–28

Confronting the world

In our early twenties we must dare to step into real life with our own two feet. At this point, we take over the reins from parents and educators, and from now on will only learn when we want to learn.

The impulses of the will are still fairly subconscious for us in our twenties. We do not yet follow a firmly laid-out path, but stride purposefully in search of experience with little apprehension of the outcome. We are quite literally expanding our world, and will continue to do so until about our forties: this is why Lievegoed refers to these next few age groupings as the 'expansive stage'.

It is through such confrontation with the world that we as young individuals discover what we can and cannot do – there is no more effective way to find out.

Case study: Richard (25)

Richard has recently finished a degree in business administration. He wrote his thesis on team development while doing an internship at a large corporate company. He was then employed in the planning department of another company, and was given the task of introducing the workforce to self-directed teamwork.

Richard is a lively young man, enthusiastic, committed and brimming with ideas, yet he often finds himself in conflict with managers. He blames them for preaching about teamwork without supporting it in practice, to the extent that their ideals have lost credibility within the staff. He refuses to accept objections from the management's side that 'things cannot be otherwise in the present circumstances'.

For example, the teams are asked to come up with proposals for improvements, but management does not know what to do with the proposals as they need to be implemented by the (already understaffed) technical department. When Richard urges a temporary expansion of the technical department, he is told there is simply no budget for it.

The employees think Richard is a nice enough guy, but they don't take his ideas very seriously. This causes him to talk and work with even more conviction.

Eventually Richard is asked to draft a plan for a new improvement that can be presented by the director. He gets going with huge enthusiasm, but quickly feels like he's drowning: there are so many possible angles, where should he begin? Which idea will be taken most seriously?

After a few months Richard has several large and small projects on his plate and finds everything challenging (in a good way). He has a sense that he fills an important role in the company, but at the same time he still has doubts and sometimes feels insecure. Is it really going well? Are they happy with him? At times these negative thoughts get him down: very few of his proposals really get off the ground, and he is either left to his own devices or he gets the brush-off. Fortunately, these low moments are brief; sooner or later another challenge will present itself, and he'll be off again!

What makes this stage unique?

Like Richard, we are often attracted to work that presents a challenge in our twenties, simply because it offers the possibility of showing ourselves and others what we can do. This allure, which applies to most new things, can be both thrilling and terrifying. Goethe used the phrase 'In seventh heaven, in the valley of death' to describe these great swings in the emotional life of a person in their twenties – soaring self-confidence one moment; uncertainty and self-doubt the next.

The great challenge in this period is to gain life experience and self-knowledge, and to feel the extent of our own limits and potential. It is perfectly normal, therefore, to have feelings of apprehension in the workplace when our own limits are an unknown quantity. Opportunities will arise for us to develop inner confidence with every success, and self-knowledge with every failure, and this is so important for later life. The development of inner security is less apparent but just as important as the external security of a fixed income, a pension, and so on.

There is little capacity for perspective in the average twenty-something, but this can work to our advantage. Most of us at this stage have not yet learned to fear certain situations, simply because we cannot predict the outcome – a quality which breathes fresh air into a jaded workplace. As well as this, in our twenties we can tap into an almost inexhaustible amount of energy and passion to apply to any new project. We can also pack our bags at a moment's notice and go anywhere in the world, as we typically have fewer responsibilities at this age. It is a time full of uncertainty and possibility all at once.

Things to watch out for

The passion we have in our twenties can lead us to commit too quickly when it comes to, for example, a job, a relationship, children or a house. This can be a positive thing, of course, but committing too early can also lead to insufficiently exploring our own potential. Perhaps we will get another opportunity to discover potential later in life, but by then we often have too many responsibilities to be able to experiment with abandon.

In the sphere of work there is also the danger that we might commit too early to what we can do well. The workplace environment can reinforce this tendency: the great zest for work, immense drive and enthusiasm of twenty-somethings can tempt an organisation to keep them in the same place for years on end. This can later backfire, both for the individual and for the company as the staff member will experience stagnation and boredom with no new possibilities on the horizon.

The beginning of adulthood can come as a great shock to an idealistic mind. Young, relatively free adults are more easily influenced by their surrounding environment, being so newly plucked from the receptive stage of life. This may well be the reason why the age group is such easy prey for dictatorial regimes, religious sects, and so forth. Conversely, while young adults can be passionate, they can also experience terrible apathy as a reaction against the restrictions of 'normal' life. This lack of interest is common, combined with a sense of not being able to connect. Settling into the routine of working life can thus come slowly and painfully to some of us.

Tips for working with members of the 21–28 age group:

▶ **Mark their achievements:** We know that people in their twenties are always on the lookout to discover what they can do – as a result, they like to win at work. It is important to offer opportunities for young team members to recount their achievements with pride, and to guide them on how to do this sensitively.

▶ **Vary their tasks:** While the drive and enthusiasm of twenty-somethings is long-lasting, their attention span tends to be shorter. Tasks and activities must ideally be varied and quick. It will really boost a young adult's confidence to see results in the short term.

▶ **Help them to develop:** Education and development should be broad rather than deep for this group. Theoretical training, or placements where they may participate without actually having a significant role, are not usually appreciated – they want the real work. Therefore, hands-off guidance from an experienced coach is ideal.

▶ **Offer feedback:** Twenty-somethings are very dependent on feedback from their environment, because often it is hard for them to gauge the results of their work on their own. Bear in mind, however, that they can be very sensitive to criticism, owing to their own insecurity.

▶ **Listen:** The way young adults look at things often contains new and refreshing elements that can be valuable. It is the task of the older team members to recognise these and not to be misled by what might be an overdose of zeal.

▶ **Ask their opinion:** Young adults' insecurity may often lead to their being too reticent to speak up in meetings. As a result, they may appreciate being invited to express themselves in a safe environment where they can know for certain that their ideas won't be laughed at.

▶ **Try not to patronise:** Many people in their twenties find it difficult to hear from older colleagues that they are 'not ready yet' for certain duties. Lack of experience is often given as an argument to refuse a job to younger people, but it is very discouraging to be confronted time and again with what you cannot do, without having had the opportunity to try.

Looking ahead

The characteristics of young adults are not wholly restricted to this stage of life. Some people continue to behave as if they are still in their twenties throughout their entire life, reacting directly to their external world without any inner assessment. This can also lead to other problems such as not being able to establish permanent relationships, not keeping to a plan, and becoming quickly enthusiastic about something but dropping it because something more appealing has arisen.

Equally, the positive qualities associated with our early twenties can remain with some individuals, for example, retaining an open attitude towards the world, and enjoying a challenge. People who carry these characteristics throughout life have the good fortune to combine youthful vigour with long-term experience, and are a pleasure to know professionally and personally.

3. Our Early Thirties: 28–35

Controlling the world with our thinking

When we are in our late twenties or early thirties, cognition acquires a more important role in directing life. In contrast to our twenties, something new inserts itself between a first impression and a reaction: judgment. This can be based more on thinking or more on feeling, but either way, assessment, deliberation and evaluation occurs – a brief self-consultation prior to reaction.

Still part of the broader expansive stage, many people call this the rational phase, the phase of common sense and pragmatism – the organisational revolution of your early thirties.

Case Study: Ann (34)

Ann works as an osteopath in a large clinic. She is married to Henry and they have two children, a boy of 8 and a girl of 6. Ann works three days a week and Henry is at home one day a week to help with the children and housekeeping. Ann has worked almost ten years at the clinic, where she has gone through quite a few stormy times.

Meanwhile she feels that she has her life rather well in hand. It has been hard work with two children, but she and Henry are pleased with their demanding jobs and large circle of friends. Clear arrangements both at home and at work, a set daily rhythm, and being able to say *no* give Ann the sense that she can handle whatever life throws at her. She genuinely enjoys life when everything is running well.

In her treatment team at work, Ann finds that it is often a struggle to ensure her own discipline gets the proper recognition it deserves. But she is convinced that the increasing professionalisation in her field, as well as its systematic approach to treatment, is of a higher quality than those of other specialists she knows.

She has regularly urged her practice to work with more transparent treatment plans, which show contributions from each specialism and illustrate a clear trajectory for the patient. These plans then should be kept in a central location and be accessible to each practitioner – not as it is now, with each practitioner having their own private file that their colleagues cannot access.

To Ann, all this is so logical that she cannot grasp why it wasn't implemented long ago. But she has also learned that in this organisation a seemingly simple solution requires a great deal of time to come about. She feels that this is due especially to a lack of energy on the part of the managerial staff.

What makes this stage unique?

An internalisation and deepening can take place in our early thirties, which tends to lead on the one hand to reduced liveliness and spontaneity, but on the other hand to greater balance and an increased ability to organise. Our emotional life in our late twenties to early thirties may still fluctuate, but it will be markedly calmer and deeper. Everyday life can be turbulent for anyone at any time, but will dictate to a lesser extent an individual's long-term mood and confidence as they get older.

This greater interiorisation allows people to establish deeper relationships (in the family and at work, for example) that have greater durability than those of people in their early twenties. They connect more profoundly with life and can take on real responsibilities.

Many of us will begin at this stage to fully ascertain the gravity of our decisions and that our choices will have far-reaching consequences in the future. This transition holds an element of crisis for some people – the result of realising that they no longer belong to the younger, more carefree generation.

An evaluation of sorts naturally follows this realisation, whether consciously or unconsciously. We will have come to know (to some extent) our own limits and potential by this point, and will usually find ourselves being a bit less open as we sense that the seriousness of life has set in.

Happily, this new level of responsibility and awareness makes us good teachers in our early thirties, as we are still close enough to the learning age, but far enough away to have gained perspective. This, mixed with our increased inner security, enables us to give conscientious direction to new colleagues at work as well as to young children at home.

Things to watch out for

Sometimes this process of interiorisation does not adequately take place, the result being that some of us may let ourselves be easily led by the expectations and demands of the world around us. Then all energy is directed towards acting life out as dictated by the social group: decorating the house, networking, going on expensive holidays, being able to pontificate about art and culture, and so on. These enactments can easily push authenticity into the background.

Some people cannot therefore move on from their twenties into their thirties. Seduced by the world around them, they struggle to commit, stick with an idea or ground themselves. In truth, they can't make choices because they realise that every decision in one direction removes many other possibilities.

Another risk is that too much interiorisation can occur at the expense of our emotions or our will, so that we begin to over-rationalise until our capacity to feel withers, and our empathy with others completely disappears. This emotional hardness may even lead to depression in some. The trick is, as always, to find a balance between rationality and oversensitivity.

Tips for working with members of the 28–35 age group:

▶ **Set goals:** People in their thirties can work independently and with focus because they are not as easily distracted by inessential matters. They can set their own goals if need be, and map the way along which these can be reached. As such, they become goal-oriented staff members who like to arrange, organise, plan, systematise and thus can handle a longer-term perspective.

▶ **Be transparent:** People in this age group have a great need for clarity. If the organisation's procedures, work methods, spheres of authority and responsibilities are not transparent and open – which is often the case – then they become restless and can make life quite difficult for management.

▶ **Allow for change:** Some people make a definitive career choice in their early thirties. This can be quite different from the career for which they were trained. Others feel faced with the choice of whether to specialise or to follow a more general path, for example in management. Quashing desire for change will only frustrate a member of this group.

▶ **Let them network:** In the context of work the general deepening in this stage often leads to a desire for further professionalisation, for example through membership of networks and associations.

▶ **Broaden their perspective:** Their greater goal-orientation, combined with a tendency towards rationality, can cause some people in their thirties to come across as hard and egotistical. Management must then put the brakes on and open their colleagues' eyes to other realities. Training courses in which these aspects of work and organisation are covered can often be helpful here.

Looking ahead

The qualities which are particular to this stage can remain dominant throughout the rest of our lives, being continually perfected as we gain experience. They can however become less prominent later because newer, more noticeable qualities will develop. Interestingly, under certain circumstances, elements of this stage of life can suddenly reawaken in our fifties.

4. Our Late Thirties: 35–42

Changing course

Around age 35 we are generally in our prime, whether we feel it or not. We have acquired some significant life experience, we have learned to know and use our strengths, and we still have the energy and vitality to strive for success.

But by age 40 some people experience a vague sense of discomfort. They cannot quite place it, because everything seems to be in order and running smoothly, at least on the surface. They expect this unsettling feeling to be transitory, but often it is not.

This change has to do with experiencing limits for the first time: limits to our own capacities and potential. Sooner or later we must say farewell to certain illusions and expectations we had about the future – all of a sudden, the future has a horizon. The phrase 'later when I'm all grown up' no longer applies: later is now.

Case study: Andrew (39)

Andrew is a financial supervisor in a subsidiary of a multinational corporation. After earning his degree in business economics he had several jobs, 'working his way up the ladder'. He has been in his current job for four years, and is married with two boys, aged 10 and 13. A few years ago his wife, Dinah, took up her old occupation of chemist's assistant after a decade as a stay-at-home mum.

Andrew is by and large satisfied with his life. His marriage is sturdy and his relationship with his children happier than most. They live in a nice suburban area, and can permit themselves almost anything financially. He is also generally pleased with his work – the director and management team seem to like him. However, now and then he gets the impression that others hold it against him that the automation project 'for which he has final responsibility' is such a mess. This is not said openly, but Andrew is sensitive to vague allusions disguised as jokes, and his boss's tetchiness when they discuss the project. He himself reacts more emotionally to the setbacks in this project than he would like. For the first time in his life he has the sense that he does not have everything under control, and he can't help but take it personally.

The recent annual outing with the management team did not leave him with a good feeling either. Members of his team and their partners took a boat trip together, followed by dinner and drinks. The whole time, Andrew felt as if he was observing everything from a distance. Everybody, including Dinah, enjoyed themselves thoroughly, but when they got home the two of them had an enormous row. Dinah went to bed angry and Andrew drank too much. In retrospect, he doesn't understand why he became so angry. When they talked things through the next day, Dinah revealed that she suspected his work was the cause. Andrew has resolved to wrap up the project as quickly as possible, and now his work often eats into evenings and weekends. He and Dinah plan to go away for a blissful holiday together when the whole debacle is finally over.

Andrew nevertheless has a gnawing feeling that this project is not the only issue. He occasionally asks himself what it's all for. Until recently he found work enjoyable and challenging, but now he sometimes really dreads it. Despite these feelings, he doesn't want to fret about it too much. After all, he has nothing much to complain about. The sombre thoughts will probably disappear when the project has been brought to a good close.

What makes this stage unique?

By our late thirties the world around us is familiar and manageable; we know what to be alert for, where the pitfalls lie, and how people are bound to react in any given situation.

For this reason, we are ideal staff members at work – vital and energetic, we have an overview, broad experience, we know our own strengths and how to dedicate them to the organisation. With some significant experience in endurance and planning under our belts, we can now also handle a great deal of work and are equipped for taking on complex tasks.

As a result, many people become more enterprising at this stage because their will has become stronger and more focused, and their sense of perspective and reality is strong. We typically have an eye by now for what will be attainable and what will not.

But in this period the finiteness of life is often experienced: the feeling that half our life is behind us. Suddenly the future doesn't look endless – but this does not have to be a bad thing. To the well-adjusted among us, the big question becomes, 'How do I shape the part of my life that is yet to come?'

People who are grounded and aware enough to ask themselves this question will begin to tackle the meaning of their existence. This is no small feat, and will bring with it many challenging feelings and emotions: the values related to the expansive stage will begin to lose their significance, but no new values will have yet been found to replace them. This doesn't have to amount to a real crisis however – the questions knocking on the door are often drowned out by the busyness of everyday life.

Things to watch out for

Conventionally 40 is the age of the mid-life crisis. And the general belief is that people who say they are unaffected are in denial. But the real danger here is letting yourself be talked into one.

Just as there is nothing wrong with the people who are wrestling with the fundamental questions, there is equally nothing wrong with the people who, for the time being, enter into their forties without anxiety.

But it is important to stay close to our own feelings of uncertainty when they do arise. It would be unwise to think these emotional signals will simply blow over. Sadly our culture places a heavy taboo on having negative feelings – these kinds of fretting questions are not supposed to bother someone who is doing well in life. Dwelling on them is considered a sign of weakness, so we are often driven to drown our unease in alcohol, dream away in front of the TV, undertake sexual adventures, or work too hard. If those determined to do so succeed in maintaining this denial into their fifties, it will eventually exhaust them.

The thought that we are stuck for the rest of our life with this partner, this job, this house, this way of life, can bring us to decide to change the scenery before it's too late. Sometimes this *will* change things, but more often than not, the issue could have been solved from within. It is vital to remember that when we move on, we take ourselves into each new situation. Soon the same problems can develop there because the problem was us, not the scenery.

Tips for working with members of the 35–42 age group:

▶ **Let them lead:** People in their late thirties are well suited to be managers. Their professional expertise – ripened by experience – gives them a real authority and power of persuasion.

▶ **Allow for setbacks:** An employee's rising personal disquiet and doubt are generally not yet noticeable at this stage, as they remain in the private sphere. But when they are confronted with serious setbacks at work (such as being passed over for a promotion), or by larger private problems (such as divorce), a temporary dysfunction can easily set in at work. This calls in the first place for understanding, not only to spare the person in question, but also to avoid drawing the wrong conclusions about their long-term qualities and prospects.

▶ **Be patient:** Harsh sanctions are likely to be counterproductive in dealing with a colleague who is functioning temporarily less well. It often brings much better results to gently remind these colleagues of their personal responsibility. In the interest of both the organisation and the person in question, it is advisable to continue making reasonable requests for work to be carried out as usual.

Looking ahead

The expansive stage, the second great stage in life, comes to an end in our early forties. By now, we have usually staked out our place in the world, and will have to accept that in the external sense there is not much more to be gained. But this is where our inner strengths and capacities will start to come into their own, and will require continual attention as we develop into the future.

As a result, the next life stage, from 42 to 49, is usually entirely characterised by a reorientation from expansion to wisdom. If it is successful, life still has much to offer. If not, and if we don't strive to get this balance in our forties, then the years that follow will become increasingly difficult.

The Social Stage

5. Our Forties: 42–49

The search for meaning

The Chinese saying at the beginning of this book speaks of our gaining wisdom at this stage of life. Ideally, we should now be able to turn the experiences we acquired in the expansive stage into fruitfulness for others, which is why Lievegoed defines this as the beginning of the 'social' stage.

To find balance in our forties, we must search for and find a deeper meaning in everything we do. This search will dominate this stage of life almost entirely, as it feeds not only into our personal lives and world views, but also into our working environments as we seek specific spaces where meaningful fulfilment is possible.

Case study: Geoff (47)

When Geoff stands in front of the mirror, he gets a shock. He's getting balder and his remaining hair is becoming a dull grey. He keeps an eye on his continually deepening wrinkles, especially the ones on his forehead. The pouches under his eyes are growing too and he looks increasingly pallid.

'Who is that old man?' he thinks, whenever he catches his reflection out of the corner or his eye.

For some time now he has lived alone in a luxury apartment at the edge of the city. He and his wife divorced two years ago when they admitted to themselves that they were making each other miserable. He hardly sees her any more; she now lives in another city. Fortunately, he sees his son and daughter, who are both in their twenties, quite regularly. But at his lower moments he wonders whether they visit out of love for him or for his wallet.

By default, work has now taken priority in Geoff's life. He is head of the projects department in the region, which requires '200 per cent' of his time and effort, or so he likes to joke. He and his staff manage infrastructural projects that juggle political interests and big money – 'we're talking millions'. His day-to-day dealings are with investors, project developers, stakeholders, and so on. An environment which Geoff refers to as 'a snake pit' of cunning and deceit, juridical procedures and journalists intent on stirring up rumours.

Without a family to come home to, or many interests of his own, this snake pit feels like Geoff's whole world. He never imagined his life this way. He had resolved as a young man, coming from a simple family of lower-grade civil servants, never to have the dull working life of his father. Yet somehow it has happened anyway, albeit with far more financial success.

Back then, what feels like a hundred years ago, he had wanted to be a classical musician, but for all kinds of reasons he had ended up studying economics. Starting out as a policy-making official, he gradually climbed up to his present position, and it looks like a promotion to director may also be on the cards. But he feels conflicted.

On the one hand the job suits him very well – the

busyness, the pressure, the huge wins – he enjoys the thrill. And he is certainly proud of his highly respected and rewarded position. He knows there are not many people from his background who can match his salary, or provide so abundantly for their children.

But on the other hand Geoff also experiences a tremendous feeling of emptiness. In all the hustle and bustle at work he can still feel extremely lonely, seeing only artificiality, and hearing only the hollow phrases people learn to say to one another. It leads him to ask himself, 'What am I doing? Who or what am I living for?' and feel used and manipulated in his position.

He is aware of his own hypocrisy in thinking this, as he often thinks of others as little more than pawns in his own game of chess. But this only confirms his suspicions that everyone thinks the same way. He used to have deeper conversations with a few of his colleagues, but sees little point in that now.

The working climate has made him harder. 'I know what people are *really* like,' he often says. But that knowledge doesn't make him happy. He spends hours speculating about whether he should have carried on busking and seen where a career in music would've taken him – whether it would have made him feel more fulfilled.

He gets no joy from the prospect of a promotion to director, but he knows he'll fight to get the position, and cannot for the life of him fathom why.

What makes this stage unique?

When we reach our mid forties, most of us will have begun to stand more firmly in our work situation. At work and at home, we are often the ones providing support and consistency to the whole team – no longer young but also not part of the older set. Our sense of reality and interpersonal skills will have further increased, so we'll often have better insight into the reasons behind people's behaviour and the processes that are at work in the organisation.

But emotionally, our forties force us to confront our insecurities and fears. Many of us worry that our apparently good run could at any moment come to an end. In our heightened awareness of the interactive maze that is social interaction, we often start to feel vulnerable. It can be exhausting for some people to maintain a tough façade once that awareness sets in.

Internally, like Geoff, many of us will feel a certain emptiness at this stage. It can seem that everything, including our own life, has lost its meaning. 'Where will I get the inspiration for the rest of my life?' is the burning question, and it will burn more fiercely in some than in others. As a result, some of us will feel at our very lowest point in our forties.

Unfortunately, new values and ideas don't crop up overnight, but it can still be enlightening to carry on for a while at ground zero. Doing so requires courage. If we make a conscious choice to see it through, then this nothingness can allow for us to gain deeper layers of authenticity and understanding of the world around us. We will see the world without the clutter and preconceptions that used to cloud our judgment.

The difficulty of this task is that the external world – partners, children, managers, a new obsession, an addiction or an ideology – cannot provide the answer. Only *we* can give meaning to our own life and work. But we will have to become progressively stronger in the struggle to do so. In the expansive stage, the soul-qualities of thinking, feeling and willing began to develop; where will they be invested in the future? Answering this question requires reflection and creativity.

At this transitional stage, many of us will find ourselves looking back and evaluating our lives so far. Our search for meaning will cause us to give these reflections a moral dimension. Questions like 'Have I been a good parent?' or 'Was I too selfish in my relationship?' will arise. Or the reverse: 'Did I stand up for myself enough?' will particularly hit the people-pleasers among us. If we can reflect without feeling like a victim or dwelling on guilt, we can gain tremendous insight and start to recalculate the balance before we move on.

But it is equally important to learn to let go of the past when we have finished dissecting it. This applies specifically to the inner motivations that were important during the expansive stage: a need to be the best, to seek recognition, to acquire status, power, a voice. We have to do this to make space for new values and ideas.

Those who are able to do all of this will find that it becomes much easier to be alone in nature or to seemingly fritter away time, and will find pleasure and security in the smallest of moments. This space also opens up the opportunity to try different things, and to find out what fits and what doesn't fit this new stage of life.

Things to watch out for

A common and dangerous error is to hold on to the values of the expansive stage. The insecurities that come with ageing can easily lead us to want to prove even more forcefully what we can do, to demonstrate that we're not ready to give up. This can work for a time, but the closer we get to fifty, the more frenetic and tiring it gets. The longer we fight it, the more difficult it can be to get this new work-life balance.

Rarely do any of us ever live up to our idealistic childhood dreams. Unsurprisingly then, most of us tend to feel like a 'failure' at some point. It doesn't take much brooding to conclude that we may not have picked the perfect partner, nor been the perfect partner ourselves, nor the perfect parent, nor have we risen to the top of our game. Everyone feels a hint of this, but in some people it can take on gigantic proportions and lead to depression – a more substantial obstacle to making something of the future. How we process this feeling of failure in our forties determines to a large extent the quality of the rest of our lives. It is at points like these that we can keep the balance by remembering that there really is no such thing as perfect.

The lure of escapism that appeared in the previous decade can gain momentum in this stage and take on almost decadent forms. Some of us may express this in wanting to appear young, flirting with younger colleagues, drinking too much, being insincerely jovial, and overexerting ourselves as described earlier. It's important for us to gain perspective at these points, as often it's the panic behind these actions rather than the actions themselves that people notice.

Lastly, in this stage we are confronted with physical changes, both externally and internally. Our energy begins to decrease, and we need a longer recovery time after strong exertion. Many women begin to encounter the onset of menopause around this time, the symptoms of which differ hugely from one individual to another. All such physical changes can make us extra sensitive to stress, which in turn can cause a whole host of psychosomatic ailments such as cardiovascular disease, stomach and intestinal complaints, backaches, etc. Any doctor who advises only physical treatment for these would be guilty of overlooking the bigger picture – changes in lifestyle or therapy can be just as powerful as drugs at reducing anxiety.

Tips for working with members of the 42–49 age group:

► **Seek their opinion:** If people in their forties can avoid the dangers described above, they will become extremely conscientious members of the team. Their insight alone can be invaluable, so it is useful to seek their opinion at work.

► **Boost their confidence:** Forty-somethings can easily fall into grave doubt and insecurity over tasks that they wouldn't have hesitated about ten years earlier. It will help them immensely to be reminded of their past successes and strengths in vulnerable moments.

► **Separate fact from feeling:** Some colleagues may project their inner struggles onto their organisation or co-workers. Their experience will give them a trained eye for the failings of others, which can be useful, but sometimes goes too far. Management would do well to take these airings seriously, but also look to the concrete facts and separate the objective from the subjective.

► **Give them space:** The emotional and spiritual questions that occupy people in their forties will usually be well suppressed in the work environment. But an involuntary outburst is possible at entirely unexpected moments. The emotional charge is likely to be disproportional to the occasion, so the best thing to do is to provide some space and regroup later rather than reacting immediately.

► **Allow for growth:** Their insecurity should not be viewed as negative but as a basis for further growth. Such a period of inner struggle is crucial in order to make meaningful contributions in the future. Goethe said, 'Die and become; whoever cannot do this will not get far on this earth.' The organisation must make an effort to help them to rise from the ashes.

► **Offer a reorientation:** An employer can help enormously by offering people in their forties the opportunity to participate in conferences, courses and workshops. Let them explore new areas, use them in innovative projects, give them another function or let them be coached by an older colleague – the result will be profound.

Looking ahead

Life presents us with a natural purification process in our forties, the negative aspects of which sadly tend to get more recognition than the positive. We must wave goodbye to many illusions, certainly, but the yield will be total acceptance of our place in life. When this is done with success, we are ready for what Lievegoed calls the social stage, which can herald new joys in the form of self-confidence, inner peace and eminent leadership.

6. Our Early Fifties: 49–56

Wisdom

The struggle of our forties is more or less concluded when, as they say in Dutch, we have 'seen Abraham'. This curious expression was once explained to me as follows:

God instructed Abraham to offer his cherished son, Isaac, as a sacrifice. Abraham was distraught, but dutifully took up the cleaver – at which point God restrained him. It was sufficient proof of Abraham's obedience that he was prepared even to contemplate going through with the sacrifice.

'Someone who matures with wisdom is prepared to give, selflessly and unquestioningly,' I was told. 'This is why we say they have seen Abraham.'

Whatever may be true of this story, when we reach our fifties we should be able to do something for others with greater selflessness than before. We have the capacity to be genuinely social without pushing ourselves into the foreground, and we can let others take our place.

Case study: Jenny (54)

Jenny has worked for an insurance company for ten years, the last two years as head of Human Resources. She is married to Luke, who works three days a week, having taken on the majority of household tasks. They have three children, all of whom have left home and now lead largely independent lives.

When Jenny accepted the job as head of HR she was quite aware that it would require a lot from her. The organisation was going through some big changes, and her department played a central role in this. At the time, she had experienced serious doubts as to whether she would be up to the job, but management had urged her to accept. Now, two years on, she doesn't regret having said yes, as she has felt increasingly strong in the position. She has even observed that she can exert a great deal of influence on the course of events in the company. She doesn't worry about her age as much as her friends do. In fact, Jenny is convinced that it is partly her life experience that causes people at work to listen to her and to take her contributions seriously.

While raising her children, she made an effort to instil in them a sense of responsibility for their own actions. When they were old enough to make bigger decisions, Jenny would say, 'I can give you advice, but you must choose for yourself.' Now as head of HR she preaches that same concept to her colleagues and acts accordingly in all matters.

For example, when a department head asked her if he could skip an evening workshop to attend his daughter's birthday, she replied, 'I think you have to attend the workshop.' He was taken aback and said indignantly: 'I can't spend the whole of my daughter's birthday at work! You can't make me do that to my family.'

She had simply replied, 'My dear Tom, now you know the company's position, you must decide for yourself what to do.'

Tom missed the workshop – which Jenny would also have done. But now it was his own decision to do so. He had not put the responsibility on her.

It is from this same perspective that Jenny resists formalism and a culture of blame in the workplace. When project leaders must be appointed to take charge of the processes of change, she wants them to be chosen because management has confidence in them, not because it is part of their function.

Jenny herself is sometimes surprised at the force with which she can take a stand – not just at work but in her private life too. She experienced similar conflicts over her children's teachers' reluctance to swerve from their pattern of thinking whenever parents proposed changes.

Yet Jenny's life is not without worries. She regularly takes work home, which Luke detests. In her heart she agrees with him because there are many things they don't get to do together, but she can't see a solution. She is often dog-tired and cannot put work out of her head when trying to sleep, which bothers her the next day more than it used to.

But what Jenny finds especially problematic is the behaviour of a number of younger managers who are out to prove themselves. She feels that they do this in a hard, sometimes shockingly ruthless way. While she is strong enough to take a firm position when she feels bullied, she gets the impression that their behaviour will only get worse. She worries that sooner or later they will genuinely hurt her feelings. Privately, she fears that if it weren't for occasional holidays with Luke, or opportunities to recharge in a seminar or workshop, she might not be able to keep her footing for long.

What makes this stage unique?

As we get older we display more pronounced personal traits. Describing general characteristics therefore becomes more difficult as time goes on. The boundaries between the stages of life also become increasingly vague as people's lives differ increasingly. As a result, we must take these general characteristics with a pinch of salt.

Contrary to popular belief, it's not always a bad thing that vital energy and passion tend to decrease with age. When we reach our fifties, we are usually calmer and more capable of distancing ourselves, both from our own head and from the stimuli of the outside world. In general, when we are less fixated on ourselves and the chaos around us, we create space for other people and become more generous.

Our vital energy may in turn be replaced by a greater enthusiasm for new ideas, and the ability to present them in such a way that they appeal to young people who *do* have the energy to set them in motion.

This heightened mental vitality we experience in our fifties can actually make us look younger than we did in our forties, in spite of bodily decline. It's easy to conclude then that we do not decline psychologically as fast as we do bodily. In fact, in our fifties we are likely to experience a new creative peak – some of the greatest artists created their most important works in this period.

On top of creativity, the most important quality for the more mature individual can emerge in this stage – true wisdom. Wisdom in and of itself has to do with deeply knowing, but *true* wisdom rests on two pillars: life experience and love. Our biography can become an immeasurable source of knowledge and insight for us, not only in terms of understanding ourselves but also understanding the outside world. A deepening of love becomes possible because its energy no longer has to be reserved for our own benefit.

Lastly, in this stage some of us will become grandparents.

We can often distance ourselves better with regard to our grandchildren than we ever could with our own children. This distancing, combined with life experience, can make us good pedagogical advisers for our children – if we can do so without trying to control them!

Things to watch out for

The benevolent attitude described above, continually putting others first, can cause some of us to struggle to say 'no' and to take on too much. This can go hand-in-hand with a tendency to neglect our own needs. Kind individuals who do so are thus in danger of being used when they are surrounded by people who do not return the compassion they are shown.

The foundation for the greatest danger in this stage of life, however, had already been laid in the previous stage. People who did not enter into a confrontation with themselves and let go of their expansive values in their forties will now have to pay the price by not being able to find new meaning in the second half of life. In those cases, they will embark on a different journey – that of the cynical, grousing and permanently malcontent senior whose constant complaining and self-pity are a burden to their environment.

This kind of dissatisfaction with life is usually blamed on others: a partner, the children, the boss, or others in the past such as parents or school or church. In short, we are liable at this point to adopt a victim complex. We could begin to feel continuously short-changed, at work as well as in our private life. Then we are in danger of idealising the past and saying, 'People still had a sense of duty back then.' Or, 'We knew what it meant to work hard.'

A constant battle is raging inside us when we fail to get the balance. We want to show that we know better or can put in more effort than anyone else. We therefore take on tasks that are often too heavy in such a demonstrative way that our environment cannot help but notice, and when the expected applause fails to come, this only fuels our rage and our negative assumptions about people. If we become like this we lose faith in ourselves and in the world and will live accordingly.

Tips for working with members of the 49–56 age group:

▶ **Value their perspective:** People in their fifties who have made the change from expansive to social are of huge importance to the team. They have a broad overview and better perspective than younger colleagues, and can use their life experience to distinguish the essential from the non-essential and think strategically.

▶ **Harness their stability:** No longer as sensitive to day-to-day commotions, people in this stage have less of a need to assert themselves. Sometimes their mere presence can provide stability in turbulent team meetings and reassure the younger team members that there are no major disasters in the making.

▶ **Let them coach:** People in their fifties are good leaders because they can inspire younger people and spur them to action. Their words have great power, and if they can resist an inflated ego, then they will be excellent coaches, available for intervention at crucial moments.

▶ **Look out for negativity:** Fifty-somethings can, on the other hand, also have a negative, resistant response to their environment. Watch out for insecure people who are easily threatened by more energetic and better-educated young people, and will try to discourage them in the losing battle for vitality.

▶ **Help with change:** It is these same people who put on the brakes when it comes to reorganisations and innovations. While people of a certain age do not tend to warm to change, wise colleagues will give it serious thought and support it if they see its importance for the organisation. It is always wise to reassure those who feel threatened that their job will become defunct.

▶ **Be tactful with age gaps:** Malcontented people in their fifties are troublesome for a younger manager. How do you call someone older to account about their attitude and behaviour? There are of course no recipes for this, but we can give some general guidelines:

    ▷ Try to break through the negative spiral by being on their side. Hostility will only reinforce their role as a victim, which encourages resistance, and so on.

    ▷ Look at their positive aspects, and reinforce them. If this is successful, the negative aspects can be discussed more readily.

    ▷ Remind these people of their personal responsibility for past work before projecting what they can do in the future.

    ▷ Give these people plenty of opportunity (through workshops or individual coaching) to reflect and redirect themselves on their own. Through talking with others, many troublesome colleagues have saved themselves some embarrassment by coming to an autonomous turn-about.

Looking ahead

It will come as no surprise now that in our fifties we can either become a millstone around the neck of an organisation or a tower of strength. It is, however, never too late to come to our senses and plot a new course, to accept our lot in life and arrive at a new sense of meaning, both at work and in our private lives. This is increasingly difficult as the years go by, because we naturally get more and more embedded in our personality, but we should never see it as an impossible task.

7. Our Late Fifties: 56–63

Releasing work

By the time we reach our late fifties and early sixties we have had a good many years to settle into ourselves. For this reason, we all bear great differences between our characteristics, our strengths and our weaknesses. In some, the symptoms of ageing are quite noticeable, both physically and mentally. Others by contrast are still full of vitality in both respects. Alternatively, there may be an imbalance between our physical and mental fitness as one element declines faster than the other. These differences depend not just on our life experience, but also on the manner in which we have dealt with them.

Case study: Chris (61)

Chris is preparing to retire early next year, as is standard practice in his company. Although he claims he could go on for another five years, deep down he's relieved that it is coming to an end. His job as a sales representative of a chemical firm has always been rather tiring, but has felt increasingly so over the last few years, even though his successor has been shouldering some of the workload for some time now.

While his many years of experience are sometimes gratefully appreciated, at other times Chris feels overlooked in the bustling office. He already stands a bit apart from the action now; so much is changing and people deal in such a more businesslike, hard way these days. What's more, he suspects that people only listen to him out of courtesy rather than respect. He wants to be useful, but he just doesn't seem to connect the way he used to.

But Chris still feels his input is vital, which leads him to wonder how on earth they'll get by without him. For this reason, he sometimes feels guilty for abandoning the company. All his know-how will be lost, and the company won't be as strong without it. He knows all his customers personally – all their tastes and quirks – and that is something! Chris has accumulated so much knowledge concerning who, what, where, when and how, all in his head over the years. If those clients become just another number in his company's database, they'll lose them.

Chris is certain that these are the things you can't pass on – you must have a feel for them. He finds himself wondering where it will all go when he's gone. Peter, his successor, is a good chap; Chris actually helped select him. But he is quite a different personality. Chris finds himself thinking, 'Of course, Peter doesn't have to be my clone... but I wonder whether his approach will work?'

In his personal life, Chris feels much more at ease. He and his partner joke that they have had so much time together they've simply run out of things to argue about. They both have good pensions and Chris is looking forward to undertaking all kinds of things he never had a chance to do until now. As far as working life goes, he has already been approached for several intriguing board positions.

No, for the foreseeable future he is not going to sit around waiting to die, as they say.

What makes this stage unique?

Around age 60 many of us experience once again a sense of inner conflict. On the one hand we have become more open to the world – we can take up a new hobby, spend more time with family, study a new subject or travel. And we have a better eye for the needs of our community, which creates the feeling that there is still a lot to do.

On the other hand, we experience the reality that we can no longer do everything under our own steam. We may often have to leave the implementation of our ideas to those who have more vitality.

But, once again, this sense of conflict does not have to be a bad thing: in our sixties we can enjoy a deepening and strengthening of our new capacity for wisdom, and we can benefit spiritually from seeing the fruits of our ideas realised in younger individuals.

More than ever before, the passage of time will begin to feel terribly quick. This requires reflection on what is essential, what must be relinquished and what requires focus – a process which begins in this stage and will continue in the years to come. It applies to all of life's questions concerning work, private life and personal development. Often these choices relate to what we experience as the deeper meaning of our own life. The process still has the potential to lead to radical upheavals: going to a third-world country and putting our knowledge and experience into action; or establishing an institution with an idealistic purpose; or pursuing a great passion etc.

We do not find many people in their sixties in the full-time work environment any more. Many of us will take early retirement, go on disability allowance or be made redundant in a reorganisation. Our ageing population may well change this reality sooner than we think, however, as more and more organisations realise that by jettisoning older employees they are relinquishing important sources of knowledge and experience.

Things to watch out for

A danger that threatens those of us who go through positive development is that everything becomes so fascinating, interesting and necessary that we cannot make choices. If absolutely everything moves us to action, we can take on unrealistic amounts of responsibility. This can cause a sense of falling short, especially because in our sixties we want to do everything qualitatively well.

Another danger is that, like Chris, we may not be able to accept that our successors will do things differently. Because of our life experience and wisdom, we'll have gained a sharp eye for quality and detail, so it can be painful to see younger people appear to ignore such things. This problem can play out in the private sphere too – watching our children raise their own children and live differently can be a stressful thing. The disappointment we might feel can even lead to some people turning away and disengaging with their families.

As with every stage of life, if we make no attempt at positive self-analysis at this point, the dangers that reared their heads in the previous stages can develop more markedly now. Our need for self-assertion can grow into tyranny through persistently giving our children the feeling that they fall short, or always thinking we know best or believing we can do things better. Life won't have much to offer those who only cherish material pleasures – they will become incapable of truly enjoying them. And for this, of course, they'll blame everyone but themselves.

As a result, in our sixties many of us begin noticing our physical decline more strongly. Complaints and ailments come, making life rather more unpleasant; physical energy decreases, and it takes more time to recover. If we don't develop ourselves enough to be wise and ready to deal with these changes, there will be more and more to complain about.

Tips for working with members of the 56–63 age group:

► **Value their authenticity:** In today's youthful and appearance-obsessed society, 'old' often means 'out'. We must remind ourselves to look beyond people's external appearances to see their value. As people age, they naturally become more authentic as the veils that hid their personality, such as trying to look cool or young, become less important.

► **Show respect:** People of this stage may have deepened insight, an eye for essence and quality, great social skills and a natural authority that can be utilised more effectively now than in the preceding stage. But only if other members of the team perceive it. If not, older colleagues will fall silent and limit their contribution. Most people in their sixties are not old, used up or extinguished, but their environment causes them to appear as though they are.

► **Transfer their knowledge:** It is so important to make older colleagues' knowledge and experience accessible by letting them write it down for their successors.

Alternately, the organisation can profitably deploy their expertise in special projects elsewhere. Staff who have gained expertise might be the perfect representatives for a company on a larger, even international, scale.

▶ **Look to the future:** It can be fantastic for older employees' self esteem to be given tasks which they deem important for the future of the organisation. The same applies when asking them to make a contribution to the development of policy in certain areas. This gives an invaluable sense of continuity for those about to retire.

▶ **Give them responsibility:** It may work very well to give older colleagues final responsibility for larger, complicated projects. They are far less likely to be reckless. Additionally, if they can set out new policies that will continue after they leave, this will make an older employee feel that they have left a legacy.

▶ **Let them mediate:** It is crucial to appeal to older colleagues' great social skills when there are problems in the team. Younger employees benefit very well from having an older coach or advisor, particularly when there is conflict in the professional environment and they are in need of tact and perspective.

Looking ahead

Retirement depends not only on the individual but also on their work situation. There can no longer be one agreed age when everyone should be pensioned off; this is no longer defensible in view of the huge variation of people's lives today. At present, however, this work-life stage tends to be the final one before the majority of people leave their work permanently. For some this is a blessing; for others it is a calamity. The latter often find it unjust that they are forced to turn their back on their work while they still feel fit and full of zest, but with some rebalancing they can learn to see it as a new beginning rather than the end.

What Comes Next?

According to the Chinese quotation at the beginning of this book, what comes next is a gift from the gods. But as retirement age creeps higher and higher, we must either expect to wait a little longer for that gift to arrive, or take hold of it while we are still working. Improved standards of living mean we are healthier and more energetic for longer, and can therefore carry on working for longer. Perhaps this will bring about a better culture of respect for older colleagues; perhaps it will improve the transition between full-time work and retirement. We can only wait and see.

But even after retiring, many of us will choose to continue our work in some form or another. The difference is that now we can do it from a position of freedom. Of course this isn't an easy process for everyone, and those of us who were defined by our work must now find a new identity. If we don't succeed, we will remain as 'former this or that', attached to the past and preventing the future from gaining any colour.

When work is no longer our priority, all those things that have been put off can now be approached with an open, and experienced, mind. Whether the life that now follows is a gift from the gods does not depend on the gods – it depends on our willingness to make it so.

Final Thoughts

In concluding these reflections I want to return to the question of how we can make the most of the idea of life stages. They are not intended to label or to pigeonhole people – that kind of thinking leads nowhere. A friend of mine recently caused tumult in his organisation by claiming that only people over 50 could be managers. He was flabbergasted when I told him that his younger employees were right to be angry! Sweeping generalisations to do with age are altogether wrong and the concept of life stages becomes a dangerous instrument when used in this way.

Real-life variations from the examples in this book are very important – I myself experienced the greatest crisis in my life not at 40, but at 33. The dynamic described for people in their forties still rang true in my own life, but it was less stormy than the period ten years earlier.

Instead, the stages in this book should be used as a means to observe and understand people better, to uncover their strengths and to allocate them suitable mentors and tasks. No one will absolutely fit the characteristics and qualities sketched out in each chapter.

The message of this book has been to encourage people to find a balance that suits each phase so that they may enjoy the whole experience. Working cultures change, and this book provides only rough guidelines for finding the balance as it stands today. The foundation for modern teamwork should always be in letting the qualities and potentials of individuals take their proper place and making good use of them. The concept of the stages of work and life simply provides the opportunity for better insight.

Further Reading

Burkhard, Gudrun, (1997) *Taking Charge: Your Life Patterns and Their Meaning*, Floris Books, Edinburgh

Frankl, Viktor E. (1963) *The Meaning of Life: An Introduction to Logotherapy*, Washington Square Press, New York, NY 1991

Glasl, Friedrich (1999) *Confronting Conflict: A First-Aid Kit for Handling Conflict*, Hawthorn Press, Stroud.

Jaworski, Joseph (1998) *Synchronicity: The Inner Path of Leadership*, Berrett-Koehler Publishers, San Francisco, CA

Levinson, Daniël J. et al. (1978) *The Seasons of a Man's Life*, Ballantine Books, New York.

Lievegoed, Bernard (1997) *Phases: The Spiritual Rhythms of Adult Life*, Rudolf Steiner Press, London.

Non-English Titles

Andriessen, H.C.I. (1991) *Volwassenheid in perspectief. Inleiding tot de psychologie van de volwassen levensloop*, Assen [*Adulthood in Perspective: Introduction to the Psychology of the Adult Course of Life.*]

Boerlijst, J.G. (1993) *Veertig-plussers in de onderneming. Publicatie in opdracht van de Stichting Management Studies*, 's-Gravenhage [*People Over Forty in the Company.*]

Brug, Jos van der & Kees Locher (1998) *Ondernemen in de levensloop. Een route naar inspiratie en vernieuwing in het werkleven*, Zeist [*Entrepreneurship in the Course of Life: A Path to Inspiration and Renewal in the Life of Work.*]

Frankl, Viktor E. (1994) *Trotzdem Ja zum Leben sagen*, München

[*Saying Yes to Life in Spite of Everything.*]

Glöckler, Michaela, (1999) *Macht – onmacht in huwelijk, opvoed-ing, vriendschap en samenleving*, Zeist [*Power and Powerlessness in Marriage, Parenting, Friendship and Society.*]

Moers, Martha (1953) *Die Entwicklungsphasen des menschli-chen Lebens. Eine psychologische Studie als Grundlage der Erwachsenenbildung*, Ratingen [*The Stages of Development of the Human Life: A Psychological Study as the Basis for Adult Education.*]

Siethoff, Hellmuth J. ten (1999) *Tegen elkaar - met elkaar. Conflict en communicatie thuis en op het werk*, Zeist [*Against One Another – With One Another: Conflict and Communication at home and at work.*]

Treichler, Rudolf (1981) *Die Entwicklung der Seele im Lebenslauf. Stufen, Störungen und Erkrankungen des Seelenlebens*, Stuttgart 1981 [*Is this The Developing Soul-life Phases, Thresholds and Biography*]

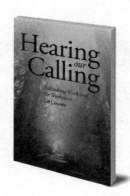

Hearing our Calling

Rethinking Work and the Workplace

Gill Coombs

For many of us, work is a source of anxiety rather than joy, and our workplace routine has become a strain on our lives. This unique book explores whether it's possible to develop a world of work which is, in fact, joyful, fulfilling and good for our health.

Insightful and practical, *Hearing our Calling* traces the history of work, challenging current work practices and routines we take for granted. Drawing on her extensive work with different organisations, the author exposes the corporate world and reveals a surprising and beautiful alternative. She argues that we all have a 'calling', and that hearing it is especially important in times of widespread unemployment and economic hardship.

This lucid and readable book invites us to think differently about how and where we work, both individually and as a society, and offers the potential for real change.

 Also available as an eBook

florisbooks.co.uk

Taking Charge

*Your Life Patterns and
Their Meaning*

Gudrun Burkhard

While the modern world is rapidly making us into 'global citizens', at the same time we experience increasing isolation as individuals in our own society. There is a pressing need for us to develop new forms of relationship with familiy and society.

Through working consciously and actively on our own life-story, we can build bridges to other people in a way that develops a new understanding for the lives of others.

The ideas and methods presented in this book are the result of many year's therapeutic work with groups and individuals. The life-stories described are the authentic stories of participants in the courses and workshops.

florisbooks.co.uk

Holonomics

Business Where People and Planet Matter

Simon Robinson &
Maria Moraes Robinson

'A powerful antidote to today's dominant culture'
– Fritjof Capra

Businesses around the world are facing rapidly changing economic and social situations. Business leaders and managers must be ready to respond and adapt in new, innovative ways.

The authors of this groundbreaking book argue that people in business must adopt a 'holonomic' way of thinking, a dynamic and authentic understanding of the relationships within a business system, and an appreciation of the whole. Complexity and chaos are not to be feared, but rather are the foundation of successful business structures and economics.

Holonomics presents a new world view where economics and ecology are in harmony. Using real-world case studies and practical exercises, the authors guide the reader in a new, holistic approach to business, towards a more sustainable future where both people and planet matter.

 Also available as an eBook

florisbooks.co.uk

The Illusion of Separation

Exploring the Cause of our Current Crises

Giles Hutchins

`This is a well-expressed book on a fearfully important topic. Read it!'*
– Mary Midgley

Our modern patterns of thinking and learning are all based on observing a world of 'things', which we think of as separate building blocks. This worldview allows us to count and measure objects without their having any innate value; it provides neat definitions and a sense of control over life. However, this approach also sets humans apart from each other, and from nature.

In reality, in nature, everything is connected in a fluid, dynamic way. 'Separateness' is an illusion we have created – and is fast becoming a dangerous delusion infecting how we relate to business, politics, and other key areas of our daily reality.

Giles Hutchins argues that the source of our current social, economic and environmental issues springs from the misguided way we see and construct our world. With its roots in ancient wisdom, this insightful book sets out an accesssible, easy to follow exploration of the causes of our current crises, offering ways to rectify these issues at source and then pointing to a way ahead.

 Also available as an eBook

florisbooks.co.uk